The Butterfly Train

A story of desperation,

determination and deliverance

Sue Mills

New Wine Press

New Wine Press

An imprint of
Roperpenberthy Publishing Ltd
Springfield House
23 Oatlands Drive
Weybridge KY13 9LZ
United Kingdom

ISBN 978-1-905991-78-5

Typeset by **documen**, www.documen.co.uk
Cover design by CCD
Author picture by FionaMillsArt
Printed in the United Kingdom

Merle Williams

Dear friend, I could not have achieved this
without your constant love, guidance and
support. Thank you for sharing the vision and
believing in me.

Endorsements

"For Sue this must have been a hard book to write, and for some it will be a hard book to read. This is a powerful, very honest testimony of how a life that has been ruined by drugs can be miraculously restored."

Ishmael (Rev Ian Smale)

"This is a story that had to be told – of the unforeseen, nightmare consequences of one girl's search for herself, to the totally unexpected rescue and redemption that finally saved her sanity and her family. A thoroughly compelling read."

Michele Guinness, Journalist and Author.

"This book enables us all to take the lid off the parts of ourselves we run away from and discover that even there we can find life and beauty. Sue writes with a directness and simplicity that disarms and engages. Her story will linger in your heart and lead you on. She makes faith real, hope robust and love accessible. You will be fascinated and drawn in by the honesty of her words – do read it!"

Maggie Ellis,
Lifecentre Director,
Psychosexual Therapist

"The poignancy and honesty of Sue's story is matched only by her openness and candour in sharing it with us. She invites us into her history, her mistakes, her struggles and her pain, but without any manipulation – she simply tells it as it is. And in the frightening consequences of her experiences, the Hope and Love which reached out to Sue becomes more real to us also. Do read this powerful story, and buy the book for anyone you know who is struggling with brokenness and despair."

Dr Elaine Storkey

To my beautiful family.

I love you with all my heart.

To my beautiful family,

I love you with all my heart.

Introduction

Many years ago my mother told me this book should be written and she was right. She usually is. But I couldn't have foreseen then that a personal crisis would be the catalyst that would bring it ultimately into being.

While praying quietly one day, I had seen clearly in my mind's eye a picture of a small boat being tossed on a violent sea. The waves were huge and dangerous. They threatened to engulf the boat. The sky was dark and foreboding.

The boat was, I noticed, strong and extremely well made. I was looking at it from the rear and I could see that the rudder was perfectly straight, and although the sea was heaving and swelling, the boat remained remarkably intact.

As I watched, words were impressed on my heart, "hold your course".

I have learned, over the years, to take notice when such precise visions present themselves within my conciousness. They are always significant.

Unable to quiet my concern, I spoke about it in a church meeting hoping that someone might recognise their own circumstances and take comfort in the knowledge that God knew their situation and was watching. They should be encouraged to believe that they were strong enough to endure the storm and indeed 'hold their course'.

Some weeks later, trauma on a scale I could not have imagined visited my family.

The storm was ours.

It's during such times of crisis that those of us who dare to profess a faith that is immovable, and fused into the very fibre of our beings, face our most gruelling challenge.

We are urged to fix our hearts and minds on the sure knowledge that He who is immeasurably greater and mightier will carry us through. We have no choice other than to grab hold of every ounce of faith we have, and meet the storm head on, calling beyond our own strengths for every last morsel of grit and determination that can be found. The fight is for real. The emotional demands – enormous.

Within the intensity of the storm, direction and focus are easily lost. The need simply to survive and protect those around us is overwhelming and it's not until later, when the waters have calmed, that we can begin to assess the personal cost.

The storm is over, it's quiet now.

Tragedy, I have discovered, brings us to a place of painful isolation. Unanswered questions and unanswered prayer are realities that dwell in the dark days beyond the storm, causing us to call into question all we have believed to be true.

Pain and loss had left me disorientated, confused and adrift. Yet somewhere, deep in my spirit remained the undeniable truth that God is, always has been and always will be, good. And because of this, I knew that, even now, I had to trust Him.

Overwhelmed by His absence, I finally called out asking Him to show me the way home. I had drifted too long.

He answered, "Go back to the place from where you started and I will lead you."

I understood.

The time had finally come for me to write this book, to travel back through the years to where my story first began. Places, people and events must be re-visited. An uncomfortable, often painful, but ultimately beautiful journey had to be re-traced. It would be intense and challenging, but contained within it lies the Truth that changed my life. The Truth would lead me home.

It was the summer of 1985 when I first discovered the powerful reality of God. I was a respectable young mother with a husband and two beautiful sons, but I was not all I appeared to be. I had a past I was ashamed of and I was glad no one knew the truth about me. I was trying to live a new life in a new place where I was safe, but the effects of my past were threatening our future.

I had spoken to doctors and psychiatrists, no one could mend me and I knew it.

This is the story of how I was rescued, how I was 'saved'. It's because of what is written in this book that I can, even now, still know that His ways are higher than ours, and His love is deeper than we can know.

The Butterfly Train

"You shall know the truth, and the truth shall make you free"
(John 8 v 32 NKJV)

Chapter 1

Steve was a friend of ours. He looked a little strange. His face was gnarled and pitted, his eyes wide and intense. He wore an afghan coat which gave off a musty, damp, doggy smell coupled with old pachouli oil. There was something about that smell that was synonymous with the hippie culture of the Seventies – and I loved it.

I first met him when he came along to the Buxton rock festival with Jay, myself, and a few others. I had never been to an event like this before and some of the bands we had spent hours listening to were performing. Their set times were scheduled all through the night, so although we had sleeping bags with us we didn't expect to sleep. We claimed a good spot reasonably close to the main stage and settled down.

The show began and as the day wore on people came and went from our little 'camp'. Then, after dark, news came back that Steve was freaking out. He'd taken some green microdot and was not having a good time. This, I picked up from the conversation around me, meant that he was hallucinating violently and drawing attention to himself. Some found it rather amusing, but I had never heard of this type of drug before and needed an explanation. Jay told me that Steve had taken LSD or 'acid' as it was more commonly known. It sounded as though he was having a bad trip, which occasionally happened. Sometimes it was down to the acid, but usually it had more to do with the mood of the person taking it.

Slightly unnerved, I tried to put it to the back of my mind and concentrate on enjoying the show. But then out of nowhere Steve appeared, his eyes wide and bulging and a look of sheer terror on his face. He dived into the sleeping bag next to mine and grabbed my hand. He was sweating and shaking and muttering things I couldn't understand. "It's ok", said Jay, "just stay with him. If holding your hand helps him get through then that's what he needs to do". Overwhelmed with the responsibility, I spent most of the rest of the night saying soothing things close to his ear while the life was slowly squeezed out of my hand.

The music got louder and the light shows more intense, which didn't seem to help him at all. At one point he jumped up, ran towards the stage and (apparently) cut his way through the wire mesh barriers causing havoc behind the safety zone. It wasn't long before he was delivered back to us in a seemingly worse state than he was before. It appeared that whatever he could see was tormenting him badly. His eyes were darting around the sky and he seemed to be in pain. By first light the music had stopped, we had all fallen asleep, and so had he.

When he came to he looked terrible. He was white and drained and sick. We helped him gather his things together and made our way slowly toward the exits.

"I don't know what I'd have done without you," he kept saying, "I'd never have made it. You don't know how much you helped me."

Confused and somewhat unsettled by the experience, I will confess to being quietly pleased that I'd been helpful and managed to gain some credibility within our small circle of friends. In truth, I was out of my depth.

However, established and feeling more accepted within this strange new world, it was only a matter of time before things would move on to the next level. Jay began taking acid often and there were times when the communication between us was dulled and distant, and keeping his attention was hard. It appeared that others who also 'dropped acid' understood where he was coming from and there were many conversations that I couldn't really enter into. So, it was inevitable that the time would come for me to move on from pot, uppers and downers and take my first 'trip'.

It was springtime and there was a weekend party planned. One of the guys had wealthy parents who owned a large house on the edge of the town and they were away overseas.

I had become convinced by now that Steve's bad trip had been down to a dodgy batch of acid as he'd taken the drug since on various occasions and apparently had a great time. I had learned that it came in tiny tablet form, hence the words 'microdot' and 'tabs' and varied in purity and power. The average length of time for a trip was eight hours.

So, the date and time was set, Jay produced a small foil package and carefully unwrapped two tiny white tabs. "This," he told me, "is white lightning and it's really pure. It's quite strong so I'm only going to give you half a tab. There's no way you're going to have anything but a good time on this." I swallowed and so did he.

Twenty minutes later my guts wretched with sickness. Then a shock of white light flashed across my eyes and I was tripping. The sheer power of it blew my mind. I was transported light years away to a world that, although it bore similarities to this one, was very different. I recognised sounds, but they didn't sound the same any more. They were intensely beautiful and I could see them as physical entities as well as hear them. Familiar faces changed and became exaggerated and misshapen. Walls changed their colours and moved positions. Everything that moved created beautiful, dancing vapour trails. Smells were indescribable. Many of these things I had heard talk of before, but now I delighted in experiencing them for myself. What really took my breath away was how my emotions were heightened. Laughter was intense and uncontrollable, and so was love.

Excitement was a constant, almost sick feeling that seemed to express itself through colours appearing that I'd never seen before; they moved and danced and had no names. It was like being on a rollercoaster of experiences and emotions all tumbling one into another. Vertical lines hung, suspended in mid-air around the rooms and they swished and moved when the air was disturbed around them. I was told that these lines are always there, it's just that we don't see them when we're 'straight'.

Many at the party knew it was my first time and performed exaggerated movements they knew I would find entertaining under the influence of the drug.

At one point amid some commotion I heard someone's voice hissing "pigs! pigs!" and I was bundled into an upstairs room. There was a point then when I felt my emotions become edgy and I had to make a conscious effort to rectify them. When the 'pigs' had gone I was brought out of hiding.

Eight hours later I 'came down'. I was exhausted and truly impressed. I would be doing this again.

I sat in the lounge with my father. He held his head despairingly in his hands. "What have you done, what have you done?" He was distraught and shocked and in that moment I felt truly sorry to be putting him through this awful ordeal. He was a good Dad and he didn't deserve to have his home overrun by police officers looking for drugs. He shouldn't have to be told that his fourteen-year-old daughter wasn't a virgin and hadn't been for some time. He had never broken the law in his life, and yet police cars were parked in the road outside our very respectable home for all to see.

Chapter 2

It was the Tuesday morning after the bank holiday and my first trip. I was sitting in school still spaced out and a little amused by the odd vapor trail that appeared in the corner of my vision, and the teacher's face stretching and changing as she spoke. I had been warned that this would be likely to happen. These 'trailers' would be present for a short while and 'flashbacks' could occur for up to six months or so after a trip. I was to expect this and see it as an added bonus.

However, what was causing me a problem was the fact that I knew Jay was still at the party and although most folks had left, he had not and neither had some of the girls. There was, among this circle, a few established couples and on the whole there was a surprising amount of respect shown for their relationships. But there was one girl in particular who I suspected would make a play for Jay if she thought I wasn't around, and although I could never believe that he would be tempted by her, the drugs and the 'vibe' could pose a threat. So I went to the school secretary and explained that I had an urgent dentist's appointment, but had forgotten to bring the note my parents had written. I needed to leave as soon as possible and wouldn't be back that day.

I made my way across town to the house and sure enough Jay was high and she was dancing and 'entertaining' him seductively. He didn't seem that pleased to see me and we went off to one of the other rooms to talk. I was aware that this was not the best time to be talking about 'us' as he was pretty out of it, but enough was said for me to know that he would prefer I wasn't around just now. So for the first time there was a serious breakdown in our relationship and I was heartbroken. I left to walk home.

I was fighting back the tears when a van pulled up beside me and a voice said "Hi, want a lift? Where are you going?" This was a guy I had come across before. He wasn't part of our circle of friends, but he had flirted with me in the past and I'd taken a dislike to him. But, it was a long walk home and the thought of getting a lift was appealing so I got in. His name was John and he had a cage-load of homing pigeons in the back of his van that had to be released. He asked me if I'd like to go with him. Stupidly I said yes.

It turned out that the place he was headed for was about an hour's drive away and I wasn't finding him great company. He wanted to know all about me and Jay and what was happening in our relationship. After the birds were released he suggested we stop for a drink on the way back. I pointed out to him that I was still wearing my school uniform and calling in at a pub may be a bit of a problem, but he wasn't about to let that get in the way. He bought a tomato juice and a whisky mac and gave the whisky to me. I was beginning to feel extremely uncomfortable and impressed on him that we should go as it was way past the time my parents would expect me home from school and they'd be getting worried.

He decided as it was a nice evening we would stop at a well known beauty spot along the way. It was then that I realized he wasn't listening to me at all. He was going to do exactly what he wanted.

I had been warned about stranger danger all of my life. I was a small child when the infamous Moors murders happened and my mother, along with the rest of the country, had been horrified at the scale of violence used against innocent children. She had taught me never, ever to get into a car with anyone I didn't know and never to accept anything from strangers. As a child I had taken this on board very seriously and had always been vigilant against such a threat.

I was beginning to hear her words of warning ringing in my ears. As we stood on the jetty at the side of the lake, he grabbed hold of me, and threw me in.

I felt the shock of the cold water hit my back then cover over my face as my body weight took me down. The water was dark and murky and in that instant I knew this guy was dangerous and unpredictable and I was in serious trouble. I struggled to the surface and yelled at him for being stupid. He didn't even know if I could swim! He was sitting on the side of the jetty dangling his legs in the water laughing. He hauled me out and I demanded to be taken home.

Back at the van he insisted on taking off his wet trousers before driving off. I was wringing wet, cold and scared. He seemed to think this was all a great laugh and I was beginning to suspect he might actually be mad. At least he was driving me home now, or so I thought.

We hadn't gone far before he pulled into an open gateway that led into a field.

He suggested we get out of the van and have sex. Horrified, I said no. He said yes and forced me out of the van. I shouted, but he shouted louder and I knew now that he was going to rape me and there wasn't anything I could do about it. We were in the middle of nowhere and trying to resist him would be futile and dangerous. I had no doubt that he would use violence to get what he wanted, so the only option open to me was to co-operate as far as I possibly could and hope he would take me home afterwards. I'd rather be raped and escape with my life than fight him and end up dead in a ditch.

"I don't get it", he said on the way home, "most girls change their minds once we get going."

"Not me", I said with more suppressed anger than I know how to write.

It was almost dark when he pulled up outside my house. I had never felt so grateful to be home. I'd tried to make light of things on the way. I needed to keep him sweet. I'd have said anything just to get away from him safely. He was too dangerous to mess with. He could still have turned on me.

Mum and Dad had gone to bed and the house was in darkness. I was glad they couldn't see the state of me as I came through the door. I went straight upstairs and peeled off my wet, filthy clothes.

I was desperate to talk to Jay and tell him what had happened. I knew he would still be at the party and I didn't know if he would be 'down' enough yet to be able to understand me properly. I called him and told him I'd been raped.

Half an hour later, he arrived at the door and I told him everything. He went into my parent's bedroom, woke my father and asked to speak to him. I could hear their muffled voices through the closed door. Jay left and Dad called the police.

The two policemen sat quietly while I told them what had happened. I knew where John lived because I'd seen a letter with his address written on it in the front of the van. They seemed reluctant to accept that he had raped me and wanted to describe his behavior as 'horseplay'. If, they said, rape could be proved then that would be altogether a more serious issue.

The next morning a police car arrived and Mum and I were taken out to find the place where the 'alleged' incident happened. They wanted me to find the pub we'd stopped at, and the field. Neither of these were easy. I hadn't noticed the name of the pub and that part of the countryside is covered with open fields. It proved to be impossible. I was far enough outside of familiar territory to be completely lost and I was uncomfortable with their patronizing manner. They appeared to be suggesting I was wasting their time.

I had been brought up to believe that if something bad happened to you then the police were there to be told so they could find the person responsible and bring them to justice, ensuring they wouldn't do it to anyone else. Another of my deep-held beliefs was about to be destroyed.

"Tell us about your boyfriend, duck", they asked when we got back to the station. Someone had taken Mum off for a cup of tea and I was left in a room with the two policewomen who had been in the car with us. "Had a row, had you?"

"Yes", I replied, acutely aware that, as far as I could, I needed to leave Jay out of this for obvious reasons.

"We usually find that girls who've had a row with their boyfriends shout rape so their boyfriends feel sorry for them and make up." Shocked that anyone would go to such extreme lengths just to make up from having a row, I argued that this wasn't the case.

"Tell us what he did then, duck. Let's start at the beginning". And start at the beginning we did. They shot questions at me for hours. They made me go back over details time and time again. They sneered at my attempts to explain why I had 'let him do it'.

"Why didn't you fight him?" they kept insisting.

"Because I was scared out of my mind!" They told me I was a slut and had probably asked for it. Girls like me shouldn't be allowed to walk the streets. They said I shouldn't expect to be going home that night. I needed to be locked away somewhere.

At one point they called in some policemen and laughingly told them about the things I'd been saying and asked them to take over as they'd had enough of me.

They jeered at me and bullied me into saying things about the rape that they seemed to find amusing. They wanted to know which bit of what he'd done to me I enjoyed the most.

They called in a doctor who examined me and took swabs to check for signs of sexual activity. "You'd better tell us, duck, if you're not a virgin, because the doc will be able to tell". I couldn't incriminate Jay so I blamed the loss of my virginity on a guy I'd had a brief fling with before I met him.

By the time the statement was written and signed I was a tearful, trembling wreck. They had picked up on the fact that I was keeping some dubious company and said they wanted to take a look at my bedroom before the day was over. They drove us home and I sat in the lounge with my father while they turned over my room. They went through my drawers, took my clothes out of the cupboards and wardrobes, checked the pockets and read letters that Jay had written to me. They suggested to my parents that I was mixing with dangerous company and should be closely watched.

In the days that followed I stayed home from school. I was disorientated and traumatised far more by my experience with the police than by the rape. If I'd known what would happen when they got involved I would never have told them. I'd rather have said nothing and let him get away with it.

Being raped was terrifying, but their mockery was worse by far. They degraded me and made me feel dirty. They made me feel like I wasn't worth their time, like I deserved to be raped and I shouldn't be allowed out. They accused me of making it all up just to get my boyfriend back. I thought they were supposed to be on my side, grateful to be told that there was someone out there who was dangerous so they could arrest him and deal with him. After all, wasn't that their job? Obviously not.

It was a few days later during yet another tearful breakdown when, exasperated, I threw out the question 'Why didn't they believe me?' I hadn't expected my mother to be able to answer.

"Actually," she said, " they did."

It was like being hit with a crowbar.

A volcano of rage began to stir deep down in my guts. How could they treat me with such contempt and disregard? They had called me a slut and even threatened to have me put away somewhere when all along they had actually believed what I'd said. They just pretended not to. They had put me through hell.

Simmering with suppressed rage, I decided it was time to take control and play this game my way. A few days later I was visited by a social worker and behaved as if butter wouldn't melt in my mouth. I cleverly painted a picture of my poor, misunderstood circumstances and managed to get a measure of sympathy from her. She advised my parents to try to show more understanding toward me and with this endorsement I was able to skillfully persuade them that the judgments made regarding Jay and our friends were harsh and misplaced. I went back to school to find the teachers had been told about the rape and were kindness itself. I used it all to my advantage.

'Pigs' was the word used to describe the police by those I had come to call my friends. I agreed entirely. Things had changed. The once nice girl who came from a caring family and had naively thought the world had good things to offer was gone.

I was angry. Any vestige of respect I'd had for the society in place around me was abandoned. I could find things wrong with every system, every authority figure and especially anyone who apparently held 'my best interests' at heart.

Recent events had taught me the picture the world presents is a lie. The only interest is in serving itself and its systems. It cares nothing for anyone that doesn't conform to its expectations, and I was having none of it.

I was intensely aware of my fourteen- year-old status and the limitations it put on my freedom. But I was a clever girl and I would find a way to live my life the way I wanted it to be. The die was cast.

Chapter 3

My early years had been safe and happy enough. I had grown up in the sixties when many changes were taking place in the world. First hand memories of the Second World War were still very much alive in our parents and references were frequently made to the hardships they had endured. An appreciation of home-cooked-food, warmth and 'how lucky we are' was impressed on us from an early age.

A music and fashion revolution was in process and, to keep pace, 'Top of the Pops' was compulsory family viewing with parents showing a mixture of amusement and downright outrage at the flamboyant spectacles. The world was a colourful and exciting place, far better by all accounts than the one they had grown up in.

Born in Derby, my mother was one of seven children who had been brought up in a wooden hut built by my grandfather. It stood on stilts and was set within a large, highly cultivated plot of ground.

My parents had moved away from the area before we were born, but dutiful and thankfully rare family visits had to be made. My grandparents seemed to me to be extremely old, musty and distant. I never saw them move from their chairs and they didn't appear to know who I or my older brother were. We had to shout our names to them so they could hear us. However there was, for me, a certain fascination about being in the place where my mother had spent her childhood.

Although a house had since been built, the abandoned wooden hut still stood in the garden. It had a kitchen/sitting area with an open fireplace and two bedrooms. Each one had once been furnished with a double bed, one for the boys and the other for the girls. My grandparents had slept in another much smaller hut further down the garden with the youngest child. When the next baby arrived the child was moved into the larger hut to sleep in the centre of the appropriate bed. In the garden was a brick built tub where the laundry was done.

Mum and her siblings were expected to attend Chapel each Sunday until they reached the age of fourteen when they were duly confirmed. They could then choose whether to continue attending services. My mother chose not to.

Although as a family we didn't go to church, I was nevertheless aware that in my mother was a clear acceptance that God was our creator, and that we are accountable to Him for our actions both good and bad. A small child easily absorbs all that is taught to them as absolute truth and this sat very well with my sense of well-being and how I viewed the world around me.

However, this was a time of great leaps forward in science and discovery and my mother always referred to reports of new information with a certain amount of awe and above all, unquestioning belief. "They (I would be told) have discovered 'this' or 'that'". I was never quite sure who 'they' were, but the wonderment that my mother obviously felt at their impartation of new truths left me in no doubt that whatever 'they' said was, without question, true.

One significant day, out of the blue she announced that 'they' had discovered we were not (as she had always believed) created by God in His image at all, but apparently we had evolved over millions of years and had once been monkeys. She explained as much as she could about what this new word 'evolved' meant, and the conclusion was clear – things were not at all as we had thought. 'They' (who must be believed) had proved otherwise.

I struggled to come to terms with this new revelation and its implications. No God? No heaven for good little girls? No-one all-seeing, all-knowing and consequently no-one to answer to? My view of the world became slightly confused and unstable for a while as I adjusted to this new foundational 'truth'.

Looking back, I believe it devalued my self-worth and brought into doubt a deeply held sense of purpose and destiny. Something in me died.

My father was a strong and stable man. He was kind and honest and could always be depended on for fun days out and ice cream during shopping trips. I had never known his parents, but stories were told of the off-licence and corner shop they had owned throughout his childhood. He had apparently been rather overweight due to the privileged availability of sweet shop stock!

A confident and talented singer, he often took lead parts in amateur operatics. I was allowed to take part if children were required. I loved it! The stage, the lights, the adrenaline! I pleaded to have piano lessons so I could learn to play the songs and we could practise them together.

He never expressed any kind of faith and was dismissive of suggestions that we should believe in anything that couldn't be seen or touched. But, when I was invited by a friend to go to Sunday School with her, he had no objections.

Her parents, like mine, didn't go to church, but she had told me about organised outings to exciting places and boys who played tricks on the teacher so, out of curiosity, I went along.

Our teacher was young and trendy and in the months that followed I heard many things about the God whose existence had, for me, been brought into question. I learned that He is good, that He loves us and wants us to understand what is meant by the stories that are written in the Bible. I was told that He is a Father, not just the Father of Jesus Christ, but our Father too, and He sent His son Jesus into the world so we could learn about Him.

I heard how Jesus healed people and performed miracles and then died for us so that we could go to heaven and live with Him and His Father forever. I didn't ever really understand how all this worked, and the general atmosphere of fun during class meant that there wasn't much opportunity to ask serious questions. But I was told that after He died, He came back and is still alive and doing miracles today. To believe in Him was important.

At home we had a rather ancient Bible on our bookshelf and I remember enthusiastically brushing off the dust and trying to read the tiny script printed on the wafer-thin pages, but my efforts were overcome by the strangeness of the language and the concentration needed to decipher any of it. So I gave up.

"Too lucky", my school friends said to me. "You're too lucky to have a real baby in your house!" They were envious of the surprise arrival of my tiny new baby brother and I enjoyed their attention. After all, doesn't every nine year old little girl want a real baby to play with? I had a doll's pram, a doll's cot and numerous baby dolls to play with, but to have the real thing was something most of my friends could only dream about. Mum and I had spent months excitedly preparing for his arrival. The waiting had, to me, seemed like an eternity.

However, in reality life at home had changed dramatically after Richard's arrival. He was not a happy baby and didn't ever seem to stop crying. Mum was snappy and pre-occupied with bottles, nappies and no sleep. She was exhausted and worried.

Tests revealed that he was asthmatic and Mum deteriorated badly under the strain of trying to keep him well. Doctor's visits, frequent medications and continual sleepless nights took their toll. What had been a normal, happy family became a tense and difficult one. Mum was short-tempered and fraught. Shouting matches, tears and flaring tempers became an everyday part of our lives. Dad walked on eggshells in an effort to keep the peace. My older brother Andrew was always in trouble for being too noisy and normal activities were toned down. I stopped going to Sunday School.

I was an early developer and by the time I went to secondary school my periods were well established. Being around the older girls brought an awareness of boyfriends, fashion and sex into sharp focus.

I was confident and popular and liked to push boundaries wherever I could. I had a thirst for excitement and a tendency to want to shock with outlandish tastes in fashion and music.

Dad's musical talents and love of the stage had rubbed off on us, and Andrew and I spent hours listening to records, working out guitar riffs and re-creating bass lines and harmonies. By the time I was in my second year I had formed an all-girl guitar and vocal group and was beginning to perform publicly.

I taught myself to smoke and worked hard at looking a lot older than my thirteen years. I spent time infiltrating the local music scene and became known to musicians and some of the local bands. This was not without risk as I would occasionally find myself in fairly dodgy situations with guys who assumed I was indeed older and not just around for the music.

My parents were not aware of where I was going and what I was doing. I used the tensions at home to my full advantage and became an extremely good liar.

I didn't expect to get permission to go to a gig in the back room of a local pub, or the rehearsal of an underground band, so I didn't ask for it. As far as they were concerned, I was either at the homes of friends from school, or at a local disco whose existence I invented as a cover.

If opposition was shown to my plans then I would fight back with a string of lies and a few carefully aimed accusations of not being trusted until I managed to wear them down. Mum was easy; she had no energy for the fight. Dad was a little harder, but both were totally persuadable. I wasn't going to let them get in my way.

Chapter 4

I had a partner in crime. We went to the same school so had lots of time to plan which bands we would be seeing, what places we would go to, and how to dress to create the 'dropout' image we so admired.

We also had the same interest in older, slightly way-out guys and my attention had been caught by a new face in the town. He had appeared recently at a few gigs wearing a top hat and clothes that had definitely not been bought anywhere near our little town. He had fair, shoulder length hair and I had been able to make him out sitting in dark, smoke-filled rooms by his unique silhouette.

It was the summer of 1972 and the middle of the school holidays. I had arranged to meet Cheryl in town and as my bus pulled into the station I saw her walking towards me with 'him' in tow. Her confident, bouncy manner told me she was flirting with him and my heart leapt and sank all at the same time.

Cheryl had a tendency to home in on 'guys of interest' with a gushing and over-confident air which often proved to be disastrous, so I'd had reservations about letting her know that he had caught my eye.

"This is Jay!" she announced triumphantly. He smiled at me and I melted. His eyes were soft and his voice was warm. He oozed charm and more than lived up to the image I had portrayed of him in my mind.

He invited us back to his home where we spent the rest of the day talking and going through his music collection. He was seventeen and had recently moved to Macclesfield from London with his parents. He was so, so perfect and kind and I could feel Cheryl's disappointment as it became obvious his romantic interest was in me rather than her.

Throughout the rest of the summer we became inseparable. I fell hook, line and sinker for this guy. He swept me off my feet. He had a charisma that was intoxicating. He played guitar, loved the music I loved and introduced me to more. We became completely lost in each other and spent every moment together.

His parents were friendly, welcoming people and insisted I call them by their first names. Jay genuinely seemed to get on well with them. They didn't object to my smoking in their house and encouraged me to spend as much time there as I wanted. They appeared to have huge respect for our relationship and I felt accepted by them on level terms.

This brought into sharp focus the floundering relationship I had with my own parents who took an instant dislike to Jay. I began to make comparisons and pour scorn on them, which only drove me closer to him and his family and further away from my own.

I was just turning fourteen that September and although I had experienced some fairly strong sexual advances from guys along the way, I was a virgin and hadn't seriously considered entering into a 'proper' sexual relationship with anyone. However, I was beginning to pick up some confusing messages.

The deeply held values that had been a part of my upbringing seemed to be in contrast to those of his family whose attitudes were much more relaxed. Sex outside of marriage was not something that would ever have been acknowledged by my parents and yet both Jay's siblings lived with their respective partners in London and there was nothing but the highest respect shown for them all.

Jay never pushed me further sexually than I was prepared to go, but the truth is I was putty in his hands. He convinced me that I was the love of his life and we would always be together. We would be married as soon as I was old enough and whether my parents approved or not we would find a way. He bought me a diamond ring. I was walking on air. There was no more a girl could ask for. I gave him my all.

Home life got in the way, as did school. Jay lived quite close to my school and would walk down to meet me in the afternoons. He worked on a dairy farm and would be up early in the mornings for milking, but have long periods of time off during the day. My school friends were envious and in awe of him and our relationship.

Life at home went from bad to worse. I didn't want to be there and I let my parents know it. My world was with Jay, theirs was built around fraught arguments, Richard's health and how much more important his needs were than ours. Mum still didn't sleep and their apparent lack of understanding toward me just distanced me further.

The intensity of the relationship between Jay and myself deepened, but I was being blinded to some underlying developments.

He often talked about drugs and how he had known people whose lives had been ruined by them. He made a point of making me promise that I would never go near that scene.

I had never considered I would, and to be honest, although I was aware it existed, I hadn't recognised its presence anywhere near our town.

I simply took this to be another display of his undying love and concern for me and readily engaged with all that he said, admiring his strong moral position.

He had managed to create quite a circle of friends in the short time he had been in town. They tended to be of the same 'type' as him. 'Freaks' was the term used. Anti-establishment. People who preferred to live just outside of the accepted norm. Some I had come across before, but only from a distance. I had admired and even tried to emulate their dropout status and hippie lifestyle. Now they were becoming my friends and I loved it.

I noticed that Jay's behaviour towards me began to change. He was becoming increasingly jealous and didn't like my being around our male friends. He would watch me closely then question me later about conversations or the way someone had looked at me. My band was beginning to get some regular bookings and he didn't like the idea that guys would be ogling me from the audience, so gigs were turned down. This hurt, but as far as I was concerned this guy was mine forever so if compromises had to be made for him to be happy, then so be it.

I was also aware that some of our friends behaved strangely sometimes. They didn't always turn up when they'd arranged to meet us and others would make comments about them not 'coming down' enough yet, or a bit 'out of it' today. I got the sense that there was some kind of code being used that I wasn't supposed to understand. One night I overheard a guy say quietly to Jay "It was good stuff we had last night, wasn't it?" I realised then there was a life he was leading that I knew nothing about.

I was horrified to learn that he'd been smoking pot regularly for some time. He laughed at my outrage and tried to educate me that this was not really a drug at all, but a quiet, peaceful way to enjoy company with friends and not even as harmful as a pint of beer. It was an ignorance of society that categorised it as harmful and not something to be taken seriously at all.

My arguments were futile and I knew there was no way I was going to be able to change anything. I was unnerved by a sense that if I didn't accept things the way they were then there was a chance that our relationship would be under threat. This came as a shock to me considering how close I thought we had become and the thought of being without him was unbearable, but he left me in no doubt that if I was to be with him I would have to accept all that he was and trust him. So I did.

Coded language disappeared. Now I was included in the discussions about scoring pot, whether the new resin that had appeared was worth the extra money, if there were any uppers around or if downers would have to do. I was taught how to roll a joint and inevitably began to accept it as it was passed around the room.

As I journeyed further into this strange new world, relationships at home degenerated further. All night parties and weekend gatherings were a growing phenomenon and I wasn't about to be the only one not in attendance.

What had been a casual, teenage rebellion grew into full blown defiance and my parents stood no chance of resisting me. They were given lies, more lies and awful displays of temper and accusations if they tried to get in my way.

After all, I reasoned that if they shut me in the house I could just climb out of the window or wait until they were otherwise occupied and slip out. They never knew where I was actually going so they couldn't have found me anyway. I was every parent's nightmare.

*I looked at the tiny, purple, pyramid shaped tabs
that Jay unwrapped from the now all too familiar,
screwed up foil packaging and contemplated the
trip ahead. This was the famous 'Purple Haze' that
Jimmy Hendrix had written about at the height
of his career. It was more powerful than any acid
I'd ever taken before. We had travelled to the
notorious Moss Side in Manchester to score this,
and for the seasoned 'tripper' it was well worth the
extra money and effort involved. But for me, this
trip was different. This time I didn't want to go.*

Chapter 5

It had been more than three years since Jay and I first met. His father had invested in a small two up, two down in the town (for our future) and Jay had moved in. I would often arrive there to find him high, drunk or unconscious, sometimes for days at a time.

His arms bore needle marks. He never told me what he was using and I knew better than to ask. His moods were unpredictable and he justified keeping things from me apparently for my own protection. The house was raided regularly by the police and I was getting tired of it.

All I wanted was for us to be a normal couple, but the drugs wouldn't allow it. I wanted him to be the guy I had first met. He wasn't and there didn't seem to be anything I could do about it.

I didn't get excited any more about the drugs. In fact I had become uneasy with the whole scene. I had picked up a few warning signs during the last few acid trips we'd had together and sensed that it was only a matter of time before something bad might happen. Steve's experience years before had stayed with me and, if nothing else, I knew this drug was no respecter of persons. No-one earned the right to always have a good time on it.

My long-suffering parents were still struggling with the demands made on them by Richard's health, but I had begun to appreciate the safety of home and knew without doubt that I was, and always had been, very loved.

Somehow I'd managed to leave school with at least a few basic qualifications. How? I don't know. I had bunked off so very many times and had never, ever done homework. The teachers had long given up asking me for it.

I knew I was talented and had tried to keep things together with my band, but it was so hard to do without putting even more of a strain on the relationship. At one point Jay was hospitalized for weeks after contracting hepatitis from dirty needles. I took the opportunity to play a gig out of town and wore a dark wig hoping no-one we knew would be there and he'd never find out. It didn't work. Someone told him and I paid for it.

The truth is, I had become scared of him. Mum used to say he'd cast a spell on me and there was no reaching me. She was right.

I didn't want to live in his world anymore, but I didn't know how to break away. I couldn't imagine living without him, but I could see what was happening and I needed to put the brakes on, at least for myself. I knew I couldn't for him. I didn't want to travel this road any more. I was sixteen years old. I wanted to live my life, not throw it away.

I made a decision. I wanted out.

"Alright", he said after I nervously explained my intended departure. "But you can't just jump ship like this, not after all we've been through. Let's have one last trip together – for old time's sake".

"Ok", I said, wondering why I couldn't just say no.

For me, a trip needed to be planned. Each one was a major event and I needed to know I had unlimited space, that I was good emotionally and had a whole weekend available so I could relax, enjoy it, and have time to get over it before Monday morning. I had a job to go to.

This felt all wrong. I had to work too hard to feel right about it.

Jay had heard that there was some 'Purple Haze' on the scene in Manchester and after various coded telephone calls we drove over to Moss Side.

I sat in the car while he did the deal. This was always his way – he wanted to 'protect' me.

My stomach churned with reluctant anticipation. "I don't want a heavy trip," I said as he unwrapped the foil package. "I'm only going to take a tiny bit of this tab".

He shaved off a miniscule edge. I pressed it onto my finger, and swallowed.

It was Saturday morning. Jay made us some toast. It seemed to take a long time to kick in.

I lay on the couch and tried to relax. A single star leapt gracefully out of the middle of the floor and then disappeared. I was there.

None of the usual gut wrenching sickness, no sense of my body surging upwards, just immediate, beautiful sensations. Jay said it was quality acid and he was right. Familiar flavoured hallucinations came and played and went, but there were lots of surprises too. Smoother, deeper, warmer.

The pace at which the effects intensified took my breath away. Considering I'd only taken a microscopic grain, I was climbing higher and faster than I'd anticipated. But I knew this drug. The most important thing was not to fight it.

It doesn't wait for you to be ready, and it doesn't listen if you ask it to slow down – it takes you anyway.

Time disappears. There's no judging how long you've been riding the wave and it's best not to try. Just go with it as it takes you higher, faster. You don't know where its taking you and you can't get off.

As I looked up I could see far away the beautiful, nameless colours, moving and changing. But they began to lose their shine. They were taking on a curiously darker hue and their movements were becoming less peaceful. My insides lurched. I fought to pull myself back together; I told myself to relax and ignore them.

I turned my attention to other hallucinations that were friendlier and glanced back at them every now and then to see what was going on. Darker, harsher, closer, menacing. I started to feel threatened. I told Jay what was happening and asked him to change the music we were listening to, to see if it would help. He re-assured me and said it would be OK. I tried to believe him.

I started to lose ground; everything began to turn in on me. I could feel myself beginning to fall, but I knew I couldn't.

I must hold on. I tried to breathe deeper and slower and tell myself it wasn't happening. Just stay positive, think happy, feel good and it'll be alright.

Not a chance.

The sheer force of the drug crashed in on me. It bore down on me and ripped into my emotions. Every possible level of fear I'd ever felt was magnified beyond description. It could do anything it wanted with me and I knew it. I didn't have a hope.

Desperation took hold and I used every ounce of energy I had to focus on clinging on. The acid was pushing me faster and harder over the edge and if I let go I would fall, and if I fell I would land right into its hands where an unimaginable living hell was waiting for me. I fought to hold on. I tried to close my eyes and look away from the ever-increasing, ever more threatening hallucinations and distortions that were screaming their way into me. There was no escape.

There was no point in shouting for help. That's what it wanted, to heighten my sense of panic to yet another level and then delight in reminding me that no-one could make even the slightest bit of difference to what was happening. This was my nightmare and no-one could rescue me from it.

Somewhere from inside the churning, mindless madness, I grasped at the thought that this couldn't go on forever, it had to wear off some time. I forced the words out of my mouth, "How long? How long?"

"Oh, you've got hours yet", said Jay. "This stuff's on a whole different level, it will keep you for twelve hours at least, not just eight."

Overcome with despair, I cried out for strength. It pushed and pushed, I fought and fought, but it kept pushing me, willing me to fall.

Eventually, timeless hours later when my terrorised senses were in shreds, its grip finally began to loosen. I started to come down. I began to breathe again. The hallucinations weakened and the darkness started to lift. The heaving energy that surrounded me slowly calmed. I came back, thank God.

"Never, ever, ever again will I go near that stuff, never in my life", I vowed with all my heart. I was physically and emotionally wrecked, but SO SO thankful it was over. We lay on the sofa together while my mind slowly worked its way back to something closer to normality. Jay seemed strangely distant.

"How could that tiny, tiny amount have been so unbelievably powerful?" I questioned.

"Oh, it wasn't a small amount," he said casually, "I spiked the toast you ate this morning with the rest of it. I wanted you to go out with a bang."

It took a while for me to process what I thought he'd said. I was still struggling to calm my mind and cope with the weakening effects of the drug in my system. It surely must be the acid distorting my hearing – "What did you say?"

"I spiked your food, I wanted you to have a bad time."

I had just been told by the guy I had given three years of my life to that he planned for me to go through twelve hours of sheer, mindless hell for his own satisfaction.

Traumatised – I asked him to drive me home.

No more, I vowed, not ever. He was mad – I needed to be away from him. I wanted to be home, where I was safe.

Chapter 6

Getting away from Jay and all that we had been together was not straightforward. He would sit outside our house in his car, sometimes for hours. He would stand across the road from where I worked and wait for me to leave. He persuaded me to come back to 'our house' with him from time to time just for a chat. It was while I was there one day that something bad began to happen.

Out of the blue the ground under my feet shifted. The terror I'd felt during that last trip suddenly overtook me and my emotions leapt into overdrive. "What have you done?!!" I yelled as my stomach lurched and the walls around me began to twitch menacingly. "Have you spiked me again?" He swore he hadn't.

In sheer panic I made him drive me to the local hospital. I pleaded madly with the doctor to give me something that would knock me out as I felt the effects of the drug take hold. I couldn't breathe and I knew I wouldn't be able to survive it again. He questioned me about what I'd taken and when, but there was no answer I could give. I hadn't to my knowledge taken any acid and Jay insisted he absolutely hadn't spiked my drink. The hallucinations eventually slowed and I calmed down. It was a flashback.

It wasn't a one-off. It happened when I was around Jay and I couldn't stand it any more. For the sake of my sanity I had to get away for good. So I walked away from him and the dark, distorted world he represented for the last time. I would never go back.

The damage I had inflicted on the relationship with my parents over the past three years was serious and I knew that regaining their trust would take time. Grateful for the security, I tried to build bridges and assure them that it was over and I was home for good.

I poured my energy into rebuilding my life and trying to appreciate my war-torn parents. They were unaware of the events that had led to this final break-up, but they were just thankful to see my life beginning to change for the better. I worked hard at trying to live 'normally'. I went out with work colleagues to pubs, and clubs at weekends. I started to date 'ordinary' guys. How clear the air seemed!

> I may have walked away from acid,
> but it hadn't walked away from me.

To my horror, flashbacks re-occurred at random times and in unexpected situations. I thought that once I'd got away from Jay they would stop. But I could be at work, or at home watching TV, when something would catch the corner of my vision, distort, and then gather a sick, terrifying momentum that would suggest someone, somewhere had managed to spike my food and my body was being lifted away back into the clutches of the drug. My emotions would immediately lock in and every ounce of strength I had was used to force myself back from falling into its hands.

The threat was continual and personal. I began to believe that the drug was out to get me and sooner or later it would. I was constantly on my guard.

I began to suspect everyone. Work colleagues, a new boyfriend, even my family were viewed with caution. I could see the menace in their eyes, I could see they were plotting against me. No-one was on my side, no-one could be trusted.

I 'watched' food being put onto plates and carried to the table. If I ordered a drink at a bar I would study it as it was poured and then handed over. It never left my sight until it was in my hand. Even then I would make sure I didn't turn my back even for a moment.

It didn't matter how careful I'd been. It was never long before I would begin sensing the threat, the room would start to drop away and the terror would mount again. I'd escape to the nearest loo and lock myself away until I had managed to convince myself it wasn't really happening, the sensations would eventually subside, and I could return – shaky and exhausted.

Finally, aware it was getting worse and I was losing control, I gave in and tearfully confessed to my parents what had been going on. I told them about the drugs and what the acid had done to me. I told them I thought I was going mad and didn't know what to do.

Frightened and out of their depth, my father arranged to take me privately to a highly respected psychiatrist in St John's Street Manchester. To this day I don't know what it must have cost him, but I knew he was prepared to do anything to help me get better.

The doctor was a nice man, very calming and optimistic. He encouraged me to believe that the fear and the flashbacks would weaken with time and I was in fact already 'out of the woods'. I remember I felt lighter and more hopeful after seeing him. Perhaps things really would get better.

In a way, they did.

All the contacts I had made and the gigs I had done over the years suddenly bore fruit, and opportunities came my way to launch myself full time into a career in music.

This was the real and challenging new start I needed. This would take me away to new places and surround me with new people and opportunities I never dreamed I would have. I could get away from the streets and the faces that held so many bad memories and give myself completely to the music I loved and had missed so much.

I worked hard with my new band and went on tour. I made friends with other musicians and artists who worked the club circuits around the UK. I stayed in seedy B&B's and shared digs with comedians, dancers and singers. We went out together after gigs and stayed up till the early hours talking about everything and anything from music to the meaning of life. We spent hour upon hour on the road. We laughed a lot.

What I hadn't bargained for was how close it would bring me again to the drug scene I was trying so hard to distance myself from.

There was always someone somewhere looking to score. Not heavy duty, because everyone had to be together enough to work, but there was always the quiet knowledge that someone was getting hold of something illegal. It did my head in. I couldn't join in their conversations, or laugh at recounted experiences, it just caused the panic in me to rise. I'd quietly withdraw from the conversation and, if I could, leave the room so I could deal with the inevitable mind games and 'freak outs' that would follow.

Flashbacks happened often. More so when I heard whisper of anyone around with some 'gear'. The suggestion in my mind that someone might find it funny to spike my food played into my fears and flashbacks would take hold. These people didn't know about me. They didn't know what had happened to me and I couldn't trust them. I could never be sure that it hadn't finally caught up with me.

There were many times I'd be crouching in the corner of a dressing room before a gig shaking with terror while the battle raged in my mind as to whether 'this was it'. I constantly lived with the threat that if what I feared had finally happened, then I wouldn't be able to live through it. I'd have to end my life. No question.

Far from it being the new start I'd hoped for, it just seemed to seal the prison door tighter.

Chapter 7

It's hard to believe that thirty-four years of marriage and two beautiful sons began with just a smile and a wink, but that's pretty much what happened.

I had just returned from a tour of the American army bases out in Germany and was very glad to be back on UK soil. Germany in mid-winter had seemed like the coldest place on earth, and night after night of woman-hungry, party-hungry soldiers, along with the constant whispered offer of all things illegal, meant I'd lived on the edge of paranoia and flashbacks the whole time. I was exhausted.

After a well-earned break, we headed for Whitehaven in Cumbria where we were booked to do a week's cabaret in an extremely smart night club. Des was the drummer with a band who were resident there. We had already met a few months previously when I'd been playing a club just a couple of miles down the road. We shared the same booking agent so our paths had crossed.

It's true to say that we hadn't hit it off particularly well the first time around. He was an outstanding musician but, despite my quiet attraction, he'd seemed shy and uninterested. He confessed later that he had purposely kept his distance because he'd assumed I was already attached to one of the guys in my band and had spent the whole time trying to work out which one.

When we arrived at the club that night they were already on stage playing their first set. As we filed back-stage past them towards the dressing rooms, Des caught my attention with a huge, warm, welcoming smile and a wink. That was all it took, really.

That week we spent every moment we could together. When we weren't in the club preparing for the night's work, we just hung out talking about music and gigs. Inevitably we touched on our pasts and the subject of drugs came up. He'd never really been interested and apart from smoking the odd joint and taking an occasional hit of speed over the years it was clear that his involvement had been minimal and inconsequential. I was a long way off divulging the extent of my own experiences, but there was something about the way he talked that, for me, made him strangely 'safe'.

Saying goodbye was hard and we promised to keep in touch. Some months later he called me to say that 'Lilac Wine' had been offered the contract for a Caribbean Cruise and providing they could find themselves a female singer, the job was theirs. Would I consider joining them?

So, I made the necessary arrangements to leave my gig-weary band and moved myself north to Cumbria to prepare for the luxury of the Caribbean.

It never came.

I had already learned to my cost that the music business is a world of false promises. Never assume you know where you'll be or what gigs you'll play until a signed contract is received by agents on both sides. Many things are discussed and many possibilities exist, but nothing happens for sure until you're signed, sealed and delivered to your next job.

So, we spent the next winter in a Chinese nightclub in the middle of Aberdeen which proved to be about as cold as Germany had been the year before. Come the following summer, we arrived on the south coast to cover the holiday season at the Riviera Lido Holiday Camp. Hi de hi!

No matter that the glamour of show biz had begun to dull a little, Des and I were happy. He knew all about the bad stuff that had happened with me in the years before, and had witnessed for himself the episodes of paranoia and irrational behaviour. The fact that he was nine years older than me and didn't have any hard drugs experience actually helped me through difficult times. He just plain didn't know what I was talking about, and that was good for me.

We talked about music all day and we played all night, every night. Lilac Wine had been together for many years and they knew how each other worked. I loved how they read each other on stage and were able to handle just about any situation that arose. I appreciated working with that level of professionalism.

Des and I married in April 1978.

Just six months later, our first beautiful, blond, tiny baby boy, Tommy, was born.

I had received the news that I was pregnant with a certain amount of shock. The strange, nauseous feeling that had plagued me was, I assumed, some sort of bug and I decided to visit the doctor only because it seemed to be taking a long time to clear up.

"Could you be pregnant?" she asked me. Taken aback, I considered that yes, I probably could, but surely not? In disbelief I took the test.

"Pregnancy has been confirmed", stated the rather unemotional voice on the other end of the phone. I was standing in a public phone box at the time and as I slowly replaced the receiver, the gravity of the situation began to sink in. This would change everything.

I hadn't considered myself ready to be a mother. Our lives were far from settled and I was overwhelmed with a sense of immense responsibility. I spent the next few days thinking long and hard about my own childhood, the level of trust and the utter dependence I'd had on my own parents came into sharp focus. No childhood is perfect, but I'd been safe, secure and loved. I questioned my credentials and queried whether I would be able to be all the things a mother should be, especially considering my past and the bad choices I'd made.

But then the realisation dawned that this little person inside of me already trusted me with his life. For this little one I already was the mother he or she needed. There was no one else who could or would ever love him as much as me. So, if I was going to be a mother then I quietly promised myself (and our baby) I would do everything in my power to be the best mother in the world.

"Congratulations!" enthused the doctor when I arrived for my first appointment since hearing the news. She chatted enthusiastically about her own experience of pregnancy and childbirth and talked as if this were the start of an exciting adventure. I realised that of course she didn't know anything about my drug related past, and was not viewing me with any kind of pre-judgement or concern. There was no hint of worry that I was only nineteen years old and Des and I were still the wrong side of the wedding day. She clearly had faith in me, so did Des and so did our unborn child.

The wedding plans were already underway, and after a traditional ceremony in a pretty church conducted by a vicar who (I suspected) was sceptical of our sincerity, we embarked on our new life together. Des's family lived in the south and we decided to make this our permanent home. Returning to the north was never an option for me. I needed my new life to be a long way from the streets of Macclesfield.

Des found a 'day job' and continued to play at weekends, We could only afford to rent a one bedroom flat, but we made it nice and set about preparing for our little one's arrival.

I nervously attended anti-natal classes and soon made friends with other expectant mums. I studied books on childbirth, and debated all the current theories about how to have a happy and fulfilled baby. I felt excited and privileged to be carrying this tiny new life.

I owed a good deal of my growing confidence to a new-found friend who was expecting her second baby. Anne was wonderfully laid back, a real earth mother and very involved in supporting new mums who wanted to breastfeed their babies. She gave me books to read and encouraged me to believe in the resources and instincts that were naturally mine. I found her consistent warmth and positivity liberating.

By the time I went into labour I was well prepared and determined to put into practise all I had learned. Des stayed by my side throughout what was a surprisingly long and painful delivery, but as we finally held our beautiful, perfect little boy in our arms we knew our lives were changed forever.

This was a new kind of love I had never before known or appreciated. As I looked at him I began to realise for the first time just how much pain and agony I must have inflicted on my own parents throughout those awful years, but despite everything they had loved me without condition. Now I understood why. Whatever grievances or issues I may have had as an angry teenager, it was time to put them away. It was time to grow up.

Chapter 8

By the time our second, beautiful little boy Adam was born we had bought our first tiny home, and with Anne as my mentor, I had begun to host my own support groups for breastfeeding mothers. Our lives had truly changed beyond recognition.

I loved being a wife and mother, and Des worked hard to provide for us all. He had made huge career sacrifices, but I knew he loved us and wanted to be a good dad.

The legacy of my past did not, however, disappear. There were times, though rare, when I was prone to periods of paranoia that inevitably led to flashbacks, but having left behind the streets that held so many bad memories and the music business with all its insecurities, I felt I had finally been able to put a measure of distance between me and a world that had, in my perception, carried danger for me. I was in a new place now with a new identity. No one was aware of my past, and by a sheer act of will, I pushed it back to the far reaches of my mind and locked it down. Nothing, but nothing was going to interfere or threaten this new and happy life I had found. I was a young respectable wife and mother with two perfect little boys who needed me to be strong, safe, and, above all, sane. I would not be letting them down.

Having my own family had also brought a great measure of healing to the relationship I had with my parents. There was a new openness and honesty between us, and Mum and I would often talk on the phone and excitedly plan family visits.

It was during one of their visits that, in a quiet moment, she produced a cutting from the local newspaper for me to read. Jay had been found dead sitting in an armchair at his parents' home. He had taken an overdose. Nothing could have been done to save him.

I sat alone struggling to take in what I'd read. A tidal wave of thoughts and emotions crashed over me. His parents would be heart-broken, his brother's and sister's lives would never be the same. He was lost a long time ago. I think they knew that, but all the time he was alive, they must have had hope. No more. I was shocked at my own sense of loss and the tears that were fighting to come to the surface. I was angry with him for throwing his life away. He mattered! Underneath all that wreckage there had been a beautiful person whose life could have been so different. Why would he just give up? But then for him, being in this world was never enough. Escaping from it to another was all he ever wanted. This was for him, I guess, the ultimate escape.

In the background I could hear my little ones playing with their grandparents in the next room and I felt a sense of relief. Please don't be shocked.

There had been times, even here where I was safe, when I'd become fearful, believing that one day he'd come after me and I'd open the door to find him standing there. The panic that this imagined scenario triggered was overwhelming and would always lead me into yet another flashback.

Perhaps now, at last, a dark part of my life that I'd never quite been able to leave behind, could be laid to rest.

The tears came. He was gone now forever, and I didn't know where.

I was a busy mum. I had little time these days to dwell on anything other than looking after my hard-working husband and growing children. I had made many friends through the breastfeeding groups and subsequent involvement with pre-school activities. Tommy was almost ready for 'big school', and Adam was beginning playgroup. Things were moving on into yet another phase.

My friendship with Anne had been important to me. But now, with our children going to school in different directions, we spent much less time together. I had learned, over the years, that she and her husband were Quakers and although what they actually believed had remained a mystery, I had always found their warmth and unconditional acceptance personally strengthening. There had been times when I'd felt safe enough with her to disclose that my past had not been without its difficulties. She never pushed for details, but simply allowed me to say as much as I wanted to. I think there was a part of me that was testing her to see whether she would still trust and respect me, even if she knew the truth.

Des was sought after by a variety of bands and was busy with gigs at weekends. I began to visit playgroups offering music sessions to the under fives and all appeared to be well, that is, until you scratched below the surface.

The reality was that the relationship between Des and I was becoming strained. He was working long hours and spending most evenings in the pub. I was agitated and aware that the flashbacks I had suffered of old had begun to reappear with increasing frequency and intensity. I was often moody and pre-occupied. Rows would be followed by days of bad atmosphere and little or no communication. I knew he loved me, but there was no doubt that my bouts of irrational behaviour were driving us apart.

I worked hard to be 'normal' in day to day life, but at night time I was vulnerable. It happened when I was tired, when my defences were low. My rational mind knew this, but then rational thinking bears no relevance at all when the room begins to sway and the nausea and terror begin to rise. There were countless nights when I would feel the bed shift under my body, followed by hallucinations that taunted my senses and threatened me. I would fight to hold down the panic. Panic was always where the battle raged. Panic was what it ultimately wanted; that would give it the final edge of power. If I fell, then it could do what it liked with me. The suggestion that I could have come into contact with anything that actually contained acid was of course ridiculous, but not to me.

Nothing was more real than this. Each time it happened, as far as I was concerned, it was the genuine article. It took every ounce of mental and emotional energy I had to fight until I could convince myself that it was just in my head. There were times when I would curl up and shake so much that the headboard on our bed would bang against the wall behind. Des would sigh and turn over, bored with all of this now, and I would take refuge in the bathroom until I eventually managed to calm down and come back to reality. Controlling bodily functions wasn't possible when I was in flashback. It was safer to stay there until it finally passed.

As far as our family and friends were concerned we were a normal couple with two happy boys. Privately, I could see things were falling apart and I didn't know how to stop it.

I knew that psychiatrists didn't have the answer. I'd been down that road years before and it didn't make me better. The thought that people around me might somehow find out the truth was unbearable. What would they think? My children were the most precious things in life to me and I knew I was a good mum. I couldn't take the risk of anyone in authority knowing in case they jumped to the wrong conclusions and judged me to be an unfit mother. I'd trusted authority figures before and I wasn't willing to make that mistake again. My thought patterns were becoming more and more fearful and paranoia was once again surfacing. But I had to hold together. My children needed me, sane.

Chapter 9

Gill was a quiet, unassuming girl and an extremely talented musician who had met and married our best man. Bruce was a keyboard player we'd worked with and even though he lived a good distance from us, he'd kept in close contact. Gill was perfect for him in every way and we'd watched their romance blossom with delight.

From the start, Bruce had warned us that she was very religious and insisted on going to church every week. This was a part of her life she apparently wasn't prepared to compromise, and had made it clear to him that either he accept this or their relationship would not be able to develop. In our eyes, this had seemed unfortunate and we had quietly sympathised with him for having to endure this irritation. Over the years we'd known him there had been many discussions about life after death and different belief systems. He had strong opinions on why he thought God couldn't possibly exist and this facet of her life was not easy for him to come to terms with, but he loved her and was prepared to accommodate it. If weekend social arrangements were made then they had to be fitted around her church commitments. We often quietly raised our eyebrows and referred to it all in hushed tones.

However, secretly, I was fascinated by her.

She never talked about what she believed and I never felt the liberty to ask. She obviously had a very real respect for us and all that we were, but unlike the relationship I'd had with Anne, we didn't have a deeply felt common cause that bound us together in the same way, so a respectful distance was maintained. I studied her carefully from afar and envied her peaceful air. I noticed how accepting and thoughtful she was and how she always went to great lengths to be hospitable whenever we visited. I wondered what made her tick. What went on in her world? What was this conviction she had and why couldn't it be moved?

Being with her prompted memories of the days I'd spent in Sunday School as a child and I'd begun to wonder. What if it were actually true?

Eventually, overcome by my worsening situation, I took a huge risk and went to see my doctor. She had known me since the boys were babies and we had a strong relationship. I knew she respected me as a mother and had enthusiastically supported my involvement with the breastfeeding groups.

Routine visits to her had often turned into lengthy discussions about the nurture and well-being of babies and young children. Surely she was safe, wasn't she?

With my legs threatening to give way under me, I somehow managed to stumble my way into her surgery, knowing any credibility I'd had was about to be blown sky high.

I felt the intensity of her gaze as I helplessly crumbled in front of her. I heard myself forcing out the words. "Teenager, LSD, really bad trip, thought it was gone, over. Flashbacks, don't know what to do. Please help me." By the time it was said I was almost hyperventilating, and I waited what seemed like an age for her reaction.

To my relief her eyes were compassionate, not shocked, serious, but not judgemental. She seemed to appreciate how hard it had been for me to 'confess' this to her. I watched her write in my notes, 'bad LSD trip as teenager'. Oh God, that was it, that was the thing I had dreaded! Forever branded, it was official, written in the files of the NHS! It may as well have said, 'This woman is a no good junkie and should not be trusted. Inform the authorities immediately. Her children are at risk!" But no, her manner was one of unexpected kindness. She gently asked me about the psychiatrist I'd visited all those years ago and how I'd coped since. She offered me some tranquilizers to take when things got tough. With huge relief and sincere gratitude for her concern, I thanked her for the prescription and left, knowing I would never take them.

And so it went on. Tensions between Des and I continued to grow, the flashbacks got worse and my inner questions about the existence of God got louder.

No one it seemed could help me. I had exhausted the options. The prescription my doctor had given me remained uncollected. What she hadn't understood was that I couldn't swallow anything that was small and round and promised, within about half an hour or so, to alter my natural senses. I could no more have swallowed one of those pills than jumped off a cliff.

In amongst all of this chaos more and more memories were surfacing about the things I'd been taught in Sunday School.

I wanted to remember, I wanted to make some sense of it all. I tried to reason it through with myself. Surely, I thought, if God exists then He must know everything, and if He knows everything, then He must know all about me and what's happening to me. If I could understand why I'm here and what all this was about then maybe I might be able to handle things better. Anne always talked as if everything that happened to us was part of some bigger picture that we couldn't always see. So, surely if I could just catch a glimpse, or understand just a bit of 'the bigger picture', then maybe it would be easier for me to cope?

So, I questioned, how does it work?

If, and it's a big if, God exists then I've been told that He loves me. Not only does He love me, but apparently, according to what I was taught, He's actually my Father, which makes me, by my reckoning, His daughter. My experience of having a father tells me that if I'm in trouble, and he knows about it, then he wants to help me. I didn't feel loved by this Father and I didn't feel helped by Him. So this, on the face of it, didn't appear to be true. So, what is the truth?

This, it seemed was the most serious question. There has got to be an ultimate truth out there somewhere. And if it's there, then surely it must be able to be found. There can't just be a variety of nice ideas that can be adopted and lived by in the hope that, when we die, we can just 'choose' the outcome we prefer, according to the convenient, or pretty, ideas we decided on while we were alive. Surely, the truth is what happens, whether we'd thought of it first or not, and whether we like it or not.

I'd taken part in many conversations and even arguments lasting long into the night about 'why are we all here?'. Some people I'd met had even professed to practise a selection of rituals and meditations that adhered to Buddhist, Hindu or a range of new-age beliefs apparently with very tangible results. Could any of these be true? Could the things taught to me in Sunday School be true? My guess was, probably not. Christianity had appeared, by comparison, to be the most unlikely, most unattractive of established religions.

These inner wrestlings came and went during an ever more strained marriage, flashbacks that left me exhausted and a very real fear for the future of my family.

Finally, I made a decision. I had nothing to lose. I decided to believe that God, whoever He is, exists. I couldn't possibly begin to decide what kind of God, because I didn't know. But I did know that, in all cases, having faith was a prerequisite. So I decided to have the faith to believe, at least, that He exists. Right or wrong, good or bad.

It was a beautiful day, the sun was shining and I was driving alone in the car when I looked up into a clear blue sky and for the first time, directed my questions clearly to God, whoever He was.

"I want to know the truth about You", I said with absolute conviction.

"If You really exist and You really are my Father and You love me, then You must want to talk to me. My earthly father loves me and if he knew I was in trouble he'd want to talk to me and he'd want to help me. If You really are there, then You must know what's happening to me and if You love me then it must hurt You, because You know I'm suffering."

"I want to be happy, but I'm not. I want to love my husband, but I don't. I want my children to have a good and stable home, but I'm frightened that they won't because of this mess I'm in."

"I want to know who You are, and I want to know what the truth is about all this, whatever it is, even if I don't like it. If You exist then I want to know about it, and I'm going to keep on asking until You talk to me. I'm not going to stop until You do! There! It's said!"

I continued on my way.

A strange quietness touched me. I'd been heard.

Chapter 10

‖‖

It was summer time and we were going on holiday. We had friends with little ones about the same age as our boys and we were going to Great Yarmouth together for a week. The children were excited and Des was looking forward to some time out, but I was tired and finding the energy to organise this 'great escape' was proving hard.

Something, though, had changed since that day a few weeks back when I'd thrown all my inner wranglings into the sky. A strange analogy perhaps, but it felt as though I'd been on a journey travelling by train towards a predestined direction, but someone, somehow had suddenly shifted the track under my wheels. The direction of the train had changed. My destination was different. I didn't know where I was headed, but the train was in motion and there was no going back.

I meant what I'd said and the strange, but very clear sense that I'd been heard spurred me on in my determination to keep asking, keep pushing, keep reminding Him that I wasn't going to go away until I had some answers. I told God time and time again that I wasn't interested in any clever philosophies or neat sets of ideals. I wanted the truth, whatever it was. Nothing else would do.

We were a day away from leaving for our holiday. It was evening time and I was sitting with two friends drinking coffee. I'd left Des at home with the boys and this was supposed to be a couple of hours social relaxation. But it was far from it.

It hadn't been a good day. My insides were disturbed and I didn't want to be there, but I hadn't wanted to cancel out of politeness. As the evening wore on my discomfort increased and I felt the nausea and panic begin to rise. I knew the signs. The room was beginning to shift and twitch; there was nothing I could do to stop myself falling into flashback.

This was my worst nightmare. I began to shake and, despite summoning all my strength, I couldn't contain it. Threats were closing in on me from around the room and my two friends looked on in horror as I recoiled back into the chair. Concerned that I'd become ill they tried to help. I'd dreaded this. My defences were crumbling and I couldn't do anything about it. I managed to get a few words out to assure them that I would be OK, I just needed some time and space. I promised to explain.

With my body shaking badly and my jaws welded together with tension, in fits and starts I forced out the words. They listened transfixed while I explained that I wasn't the person they thought they knew, that I'd been mixed up in drugs as a teenager and something bad had happened to me. I'd had these flashbacks ever since. I told them I'd tried to get help, but no-one knew what to do and I was losing ground. I'd exhausted my options and was now asking God to help me.

Wide-eyed, they listened as I used every last bit of energy I had to make what felt like a final, desperate statement.

"I've had enough of this! I'm at the end of myself! I've told God that if He exists then I want to know about it. I'm not going to wait till I'm on my deathbed before I start asking Him to help me. If He's really there and if Jesus Christ really is who He said He was then I need Him, and I need Him right now because I can't go on another day like this!" I meant every word.

A disturbed, sleepless night followed and Des left early the next morning for work. The plan was that by the time he returned the suitcases would be packed, ready to be loaded into the car so we could get an early start the following morning.

I sat on the floor of the lounge in my dressing gown and contemplated what was ahead. I was tired, drained and upset. My cover was blown. The truth was out and I felt beaten. I looked around tearfully at the piles of washing to be sorted through, the sink full of dirty dishes and a hundred-and-one jobs that needed to be done. I didn't have the will or the energy to go on holiday.

Suddenly I had a strange sense that I wasn't alone. Someone was with me. "It's alright, Sue." I 'felt' the words inside me. "Just move that pile of clothes over there and take that other pile to the washing machine." I felt a 'lifting' inside as I responded. More words came, and as I continued to listen and follow their lead a strange kind of energy began to bubble inside of me. The more I listened, the lighter I felt. Puzzled, I continued to follow the instructions and was amazed to find that every now and then my insides seemed to leap with excitement.

By the time Des arrived home, the packing was done, the house was clean and tidy, the boys were all ready and dinner was on the way. I chatted enthusiastically to him about what a wonderful day we'd had, and as I cooked I felt a sense of pride and privilege to be cooking for my man.

The next morning we got up bright and early to set off. I was energised and excited! We sang songs along the way. I looked around at the countryside and really began to take in just how beautiful it was. "How amazing that all of this could be created," I thought. (What was that? Created? Who says? said my upbringing.) "Yes, created," I countered. Joy hugged my insides.

I looked over at Des as he sat in the driver's seat. "Isn't he wonderful?" I thought. "He's my husband, he's the father of my children and I love him.." Where did that come from? said the other me. What on earth is happening to me? were the thoughts that kept presenting themselves in my mind. "Could this be God? Could it be Him?" Another leap of excitement.

We arrived in Great Yarmouth with our friends following close behind and we began a wonderful holiday. Des was like a dog with two tails. Here was a woman who only a few days ago had hardly been speaking to him who now couldn't do enough for him! The children were happy and enjoying the fact that Mum had lots more energy than usual to play and join in the fun.

All the time I was silently communicating with this new 'someone'. There were no words as such, just clear impressions of a 'higher presence' so kind, strong, gentle and so 'true'.

Truth was the overwhelming sense that seemed to be at the core of everything I was experiencing. How can anyone describe what it feels like to be inside of truth? There was a purity, an absoluteness, a 'knowing' somewhere deep inside that everything in its reality is already 'known'. There was a sense of being joined somehow to this wonderful, safe, forever person from whom nothing was hidden.

We were days into our holiday and all on the beach together. I'd had a growing sense of anticipation all day and my stomach felt like it was housing a thousand butterflies. As I ran along the shore trying to work out the puzzle, I looked into the clear blue sky and once again threw my questions at God. "OK, what is it?" I said. "What's going on? I need to know what this is all about!" As I stared into the sky I knew, I just knew with everything in me, that Jesus was alive. I couldn't see Him in the sense that we would normally understand, but I knew He was there, I knew I was speaking directly to Him. "It's You, isn't it?" I said, laughing and crying with delight "It really is You, Jesus. You really are alive!" The anticipation inside of me exploded and I was overwhelmed by a pure, beautiful joy. The silent voice that I'd 'felt' so many times over the past week or so suddenly spoke audibly into my ear.

"You're born again, you're born again." I'd heard that phrase somewhere before.

Now the communication between us was stronger and clearer. I was being given an opportunity to live my life in a new way. We 'talked together' silently while ordinary conversations were going on around me. Sometimes I was able to add things in that He was impressing on me. I was amazed at how, if this happened, people would open up and honest, real issues would get talked about and sometimes even resolved.

Our friends were asking, "What's going on with you? You're different. It's as if you're intoxicated, but you don't drink." It was true, I never touched alcohol, ever.

I couldn't risk the effect it might have on me. And in case you were wondering what happened to the flashbacks, they were strangely, but wonderfully absent.

It didn't last.......

They were back, big time. More intense than ever, and more often than ever. I tried so hard to hold myself back from them, but I couldn't. They were so strong and almost vengeful in their ferocity. It was as if a huge black cloud had engulfed me and I couldn't find my way out.

I was scared.......really scared.

Chapter 11

Our holiday had been wonderful and we'd arrived home happier than we'd been for a long time. I was full of joy and real hope for the future. I'd discovered that Jesus Christ was alive and had personally shown me that somehow a new life, living His way, was mine for the taking. I'd been given a second chance to live, His way, with Him. It had been hard to get my head around what was happening and I still didn't understand any of it. But stories and scriptures I'd heard all those years ago were crashing back into my mind and seemed to leap into life. Suddenly it was all so very important, but I hadn't ever realised it until now.

He told me that it wouldn't be easy. I didn't understand.

I'd fallen in love with Des all over again, and I'd seen that marrying him and having our two amazing children had been no accident. God had planned for us all to be together from the start. There was a plan? Yes, a plan.

But only days after we'd arrived home the excitement began to fade. I didn't want to acknowledge it, but the elation I'd felt was getting 'thinner' and that very genuine new smile I had constantly worn became forced and empty. I was losing the ability to hear Him or sense His closeness.

Des went back to work and I began to feel the threat return. There was a menace in the air and I could feel myself falling.

I used all the energy I had to try and keep what I'd found, but it was like trying to grip hold of a handful of sand. The harder I tried the more it just kept leaking out, and fear began to whisper again.

I tried to ignore it. I tried to hold out believing that I'd found God and He was in charge now. Surely with Him on my side I didn't need to worry about any of that stuff any more, did I?

I called out to Him, but He wasn't there. I prayed, but there was no response.

The flashbacks kicked in like I'd never known before. So deep and intense. No sooner did one begin to calm and start to level out when I could sense another coming up behind. There was no mercy. It was personal.

Tom was getting ready to go back to school and Adam was beginning playschool. Things needed to be done and put in place for them, but it was hard to focus. The relationship between Des and I just disintegrated and there were times when we barely even acknowledged each other.

A huge black cloud had engulfed me and no matter which way I turned there seemed to be no way out. I was confused and scared.

In desperation I drove over to see Anne. Would she be able to offer any help? As always her kitchen door was wide open and she was busy inside with her youngest baby. She wasn't expecting me and looked shocked as I stood in the doorway. She could see something was wrong. I tearfully explained what had happened on our holiday and the devastating turn of events since. "I thought I'd found God", I said, "but He's not there any more and I can't cope with what's happening to me." She listened intently and I was grateful for her love and concern, but she didn't have any answers; no one did.

As the days passed by it got worse. I felt as if I was on a battlefield fighting for my life and I was running out of energy. My enemy was getting stronger and I kept reaching out hoping that God just might be there to help me, but He never was.

"I found God", I kept trying to tell myself. "He heard me, He spoke to me. Where is He, why isn't He helping me? …. Perhaps He is helping me, even now, but it's just that I can't feel it. Perhaps I just have to wait." The arguments went round and round in my head.

Two words dropped into my mind seemingly from nowhere, "have faith".

"OK….I'm going to believe that He IS there and that He IS helping me even though I can't see it and I can't feel it. I have no choice, I have to trust Him." Grasping at anything I could to try to ward off the terror I began to sing. I didn't know any of the songs that people sang in church, but I did know Amazing Grace so I sang it as loudly as I could, over and over again. For a while, it helped.

But eventually its calming effect was lost. I was going down. My energy was spent, I was losing my sanity. What would happen to my beautiful boys when I finally broke? Who would love them, take care of them? The thought that they would have to be told I couldn't be there for them any more was unbearable.

Where would I be taken? What would happen to me? Perhaps I was in such a bad way that even God couldn't help me.

That must be it, that's why He's not here. Even He can't help me.

I was at the end of the road and I knew it. I had lost the fight.

Exhausted and beaten I took myself into the bathroom just to get a few minutes space. The boys were downstairs playing and I couldn't function any more. I sat on the loo with my head in my hands and contemplated the inevitable breakdown. I reached out to God one last desperate time, and prayed like I'd never prayed before.

"Please God", I cried, "Please help me, I thought I'd found You, I thought You were there, but I can't hear You any more. If You really are there then please come now to help me. I can't go on another minute and I'm so frightened for my children."

Something happened.

Deep down in the pit of my stomach I felt something stir. It was very faint, but it caught my attention. I had to concentrate. Was it God? I didn't know, but I was desperate enough to hope it might be. There was no comparison to be made between this and what I'd felt weeks before when I'd met with Jesus.

That was a bubbly, happy and overwhelmingly exciting experience. This was deep and serious and it was difficult for me to connect with it. But as I tried, images appeared in my mind of that dreadful day all those years ago with Jay when that acid trip went so out of control. Quietly, from deep inside that slow stirring, two words were spoken. "Forgive him."

What? Had I heard something? No, surely not, that can't be right, it makes no sense. God knows I've been like this for eleven years because of what he did on that day! Confused, I went back to question what I'd heard. There was silence, no response – except a sense that this was non-negotiable.

I had to think. If this was God, and I didn't know if it was, then what I was being asked to do must be important. I had to find a way. I actually had to find inside of myself something called forgiveness for someone who had ruined my life and who wasn't even here for me to forgive. How could I do that?

I guessed that if this was for real, then simple words would not be enough. Something real and genuine was required. So I began to search. It was hard and it took a long time. How does anyone find, then recognise forgiveness, and then know what to do with it?

After some intense inner searching and holding what felt like the tiniest pinprick of something I hoped was forgiveness, and conscious that I was still taking a chance on this being God, I could do nothing else, but offer it to Him.

"Lord, I don't understand any of this and I don't know where Jay is, but I know You do, so all I can do is give this to You. Here's my forgiveness, please take it for him."

A moment later something inside of me shifted, then it shifted again. From deep down in the pit of my stomach something began to move up through my body. It kept rising.

I gasped as I felt it gather speed and move all the way up then leave through the back of my neck. It just flew away.

As it left something else began to happen in my legs. It was as if someone was pouring water into me like I was an empty vase. It was bubbling up through my legs. It was laughing and dancing and chattering with words I couldn't understand. It got louder as it bubbled up through my body and I drew back as it approached my chest, concerned I might drown in it. But then, as it reached my heart I found I could understand some of the words. They said, "There's no room for hate." Then it filled me right to the top of my head and rested. There was complete stillness, complete peace.

I was in the presence of God. He was right there with me, in me. I knew in that moment that I would live forever in eternity with Him. I knew He loved me more than I could ever have imagined and He had watched and waited all of my life for this moment. He knew it would come, and I felt His joy. Every need I'd ever had was completely fulfilled in that moment. He was holy, a King above every king that had ever existed on the face of the earth. He was the Lord God Almighty and no power in heaven or earth could touch Him. He was limitless, complete, vast, eternal.

There are no words I can write that can begin to express what those few moments were like. He held the past, present and future of the whole of mankind in His hands and yet He'd taken the time to be with me through all the years of my life and I hadn't known it till now. Even on that awful day eleven years ago when everything went so wrong He hadn't left me, and He'd been with me through all the terror times since. He knew me so well. He was the God who has been spoken of throughout the ages, the Lord who spoke to Moses and parted the Red Sea, He'd walked on the earth, performed miracles and healed the sick. He was the God of Abraham, Isaac and Jacob and He was the God of me. All that I had ever been was known by Him and my life, for all eternity was safe in His hands..

Something very dark and very bad had lived inside of me all of those years. Now it was gone forever. I knew it would never come back.

It was a long time before I was able to move from that tiny room. I stood slowly. My body felt strange and new. I was light, clean, unfamiliar with myself. I was in shock.

I needed to see if the boys were alright. They were playing quietly downstairs. I didn't know how long I'd been away from them, but they were fine, they hadn't needed me. God's presence was tangible in the room where they played and throughout the whole house.

When I climbed into bed that night the sense of pure peace was overwhelming. This time of the day was always the worst for me. This was when the threats really stepped up. But tonight was quiet, calm and eternally safe. I knew from now on it always would be. Peace lay with me as I placed my head on the pillow and was still there when I opened my eyes the next morning. He would always be there.

When Des arrived home the following evening I finally managed to speak. "Something amazing has happened," I said quietly and calmly, "God has spoken to me, He's done something to me and everything's changed. It's all gone, He's taken all that bad stuff away from me. He really is there, it's all true. Everything we were ever told about Him is true."

He listened and tried to be supportive, but I could see that he was more seriously concerned for me than he was believing of me. I couldn't blame him for being alarmed, after all I'd been pretty well ready to go over the edge for a long time. Perhaps now his fears had finally been realised and I'd actually snapped. But that was OK. I knew I was more sane now than I'd ever been in my life. I didn't need to worry about him. He would know the truth in time. God would show him.

The days that followed were a blissful mix of awe and exploration. I was completely lost in the wonder and glory of God. Many times I fell to my knees in worship, overwhelmed by His love, His closeness, His might. I was grateful, thankful, joyful, beautifully broken and humbled beyond words. He was God of the Ages and He was my friend. He could hold the whole universe together and yet at the same time be with me as if I were the only one here. I asked Him about so many things. I was like a little child who wanted the answers to more questions than was good for me to know, and I could feel His pleasure.

Each time I thought of Jay I was overwhelmed with compassion for him. I'd had no idea that unforgiveness had been a factor that had bound me to him and the awful events of eleven years ago. I felt ashamed that I'd been capable of actually hating someone, even worse that I hadn't even recognised it in myself.

I wanted so much to make things right for him, but I couldn't. I had to leave him in the hands of this wonderful, compassionate, glorious, all powerful, all seeing and all knowing God who forgives, and loves, and lives on an unlimited eternal scale that we can't even begin to grasp. He can be completely trusted with all things past, present and future.

I was learning so much, but there was still so much I didn't understand. How was this possible? Why me? Why had I been allowed to glimpse such power and holiness and be changed so incredibly? Are there other people out there who know God like this? Surely there must be or is it just me? Have I been chosen? Is there something I'm meant to do here on earth that I'm being prepared for? Whoa, whoa, this was all getting too much for me to cope with. I needed to talk to someone.

I needed to talk to Gill.

Chapter 12

I begged Des to call Bruce and arrange for us to visit them.
Sunday lunch was duly booked and I counted off the days.
"Would Gill understand? Would she know what I was talking
about? What if she didn't? What then? Am I a Christian, or
something else?" No, there was no mistaking who I'd met. I
surely must be a Christian. It felt right.

"I have something to tell you", I began nervously when
we finally had a moment alone together. She shrieked with
joy and hugged me as I told her that I'd found God. "Tell me,
what's happened?" she asked, "Who are your friends?"

"Friends?" I said, "What do you mean?"

She listened intently as I recounted the events that had
taken place over the last few months. She was visibly shocked
when I told her about what God had done, how He'd set me
free and spoken so clearly and beautifully to me.

That day we spent together is one I will never forget. The
sheer relief of being able to offload everything, the whole
story, to someone who actually knew God, was wonderful.
She questioned me over and over again taking absolute delight
in every detail. She was shocked to learn about my past and
how, although she'd known me for some time now, had never
been aware of my inner struggles.

She seemed to find the fact that I didn't know any Christians
particularly intriguing. I couldn't quite understand why. It

wasn't until much later that I began to realise my particular journey to faith was, by all accounts, unusual.

When lunch was over she produced a Bible and began to show me passages that corresponded with the experiences I was recounting to her. I was overwhelmed with what she read to me. I didn't own a Bible of my own so she gave me one of her spare copies. I was desperate to read about Jesus and the time He had spent here on the earth. I still needed to more fully understand how it was that all this had been made possible through His death on the cross. I was thirsty for knowledge, hungry for the food that was contained within its pages.

Opening it for myself for the first time was truly awesome. I felt the Holy Spirit inside of me leap as I began to read. Everything seemed uncannily familiar. It was as if the Spirit already knew exactly what was written and as my eyes fell on the passages I felt strangely acquainted with them. I consumed the book of Acts like a hungry child. The work of the Holy Spirit after Jesus had ascended into Heaven was immediately relevant to everything I had experienced. I was intrigued by what happened to the disciples when they gathered together in the upper room. I identified with Paul in his encounter with Jesus on the road to Damascus, and delighted in the course of events that changed him from a persecutor of Christians into the greatest apostle the world has ever known. What an awesome, incredible account of God's power and love!

Gill and I met regularly and became the closest of friends. Her years of experience in walking with God were like gold to me. I grilled her for hours about scriptures I'd read, but not been able to understand. She supplied me with books and teachings and took me along to her church.

Des and Bruce were left to juggle dinner and child-care while we sang and prayed and talked our way through Sunday after Sunday.

She wisely advised me to look for a church close to our home where I could forge relationships with Christians who would become part of my life on a more day-to-day basis. She was right, of course, but I didn't know where to start.

I had already made a Sunday morning visit to the Church where Des and I had been married. I went full of anticipation to see if God was there. The same vicar was in situ and although I appreciated the skill of his sermon, I'd left feeling frustrated and let down.

My dear friend Anne was wonderfully encouraged and challenged by the change in me. We talked for hours about what had happened and I asked if I could come along to one of her Quaker meetings where everyone sat in silence and 'waited for God'. This again filled me with anticipation, but one visit was enough for me. I wanted to sing and shout love and gratitude to my beautiful, wonderful God! Amused, we realised that this kind of outburst wouldn't have gone down well at all and we agreed that hers wasn't the best direction for me.

I was about to see, yet again, that God had a plan.

Each afternoon Adam and I would stand outside our small village school and wait for Tom to emerge tired and slightly dishevelled after a day's activities. I had known many of the other mums from toddler and playgroup days and so chatting outside the school gates came easily. However, I found I was becoming acutely aware of certain mums who up until then, although I had known them vaguely, hadn't particularly registered among my closer acquaintances. God's quiet, but sure leading was unmistakable.

"That's My child", He would say as my eyes fell in a particular direction. "That's My child, talk to her." And as the days went by, one by one He pointed out a whole group of fellow mums to me.

Nervously I edged myself into conversation with them hoping for an opportunity to 'test the water'. I was looking for something, anything that would open the way for me and confirm that they did indeed belong to God. I managed, during one slightly forced conversation, to make a rather stumbling (as I remember, out of context) comment regarding faith, which caught their attention. Within just a few days I was 'outed' and welcomed into a previously unknown circle of wonderful, strong, women of God who took me under their wing and are still, to this day, among my closest friends.

I spent the next three months sitting at the back of their church crying with joy. How wonderful it was to be with people who knew God, who sang songs of love and worship to Him, who talked to Him and about Him with the same wonder and adoration that I felt and simply could not contain.

I went along to wonderful gatherings of women who talked and prayed and sang together about His love. Gill came over often and accompanied me to many such meetings. I was being grounded and taught in the things of God and it felt like my heart was on fire.

I talked with my mother on the phone about what had happened. She had been blissfully unaware of how intense the ongoing struggle with my past had been, and hearing about the extent of my anguish followed by my eventual encounter with God was more than a little overwhelming for her. However, years later, with her own childhood faith re-awakened, she and I prayed together for Christ to intervene in her life, and she too came to know the touch of His love.

It was two years after my own conversion that Des finally gave in. It's true that he'd been sceptical and dismissive at first, but I'd known it would only be a matter of time before he'd run out of alternative explanations and arguments for my new found peace. No one can fight the love of Jesus for long. Did you know you can love someone to death? I knew that all I needed to do was love him God's way and in the end he'd give up and give in. He did.

I delighted in watching our two little boys respond to the Holy Spirit as He gently drew them. They arrived in faith well before their dad, and I wasn't surprised. Children have a wonderful, uncomplicated way of recognising love and truth.

I learned too, through the years that followed, that God doesn't waste anything. He brings to the fore everything He has built into us, and He uses all that life has presented us with, both good and bad to shape and grow us.

Music was, and always had been, at our core and it wasn't long before both Des and I recognised that God was calling us to use our gifts to draw people closer to Him.

I had at first questioned why God should need to single out individuals from within His church to 'lead' others into a closeness with Him. Surely those who know God need little encouragement when it comes to focussing their minds and hearts on His immense power and love for them? What need had He of platforms and PA systems? He answered by placing a clearly defined picture into my mind. I saw a pilot plane leading a glider gently and safely into the sky.

"As the plane tows the glider upwards, so it is your role to lead my people into my presence," He told me. "When they're there, let go, and I will guide them by my Spirit."

So, we joined together with Gill and other talented musicians and for years we visited churches and played at events throughout the UK leading and supporting God's people as they lifted their hearts and voices to Him in worship.

It was some years later when I was involved in leading a local women's group that I became aware of a further, yet unresolved inner struggle. A woman previously unknown to me had joined the leadership team. She was a Police Chief Superintendent and it took me a while to realise that her presence was causing me to feel anxious and threatened.

I recognised that the time had come for me to finally deal with the legacy of the rape. Sarah was strong, kind and wise. She sat quietly with me one day while I recounted the events that had led to a deep-rooted mistrust and disrespect. Every bit of suppressed anger, pain and resentment I had harboured came surging out of my insides, no holds barred.

She talked with me for a long time about how clumsy and ignorant the treatment of rape victims had been back in those days, and how much attention has since been given to specialised training within the service. There was now, she assured me, a much greater awareness and understanding of sexual crime and how to care for its victims. She apologised to me personally for the barbaric treatment I had received and we prayed together, releasing the whole sorry mess safely into God's hands.

Years later, I find myself working closely with a specialist organisation supporting men, women and children who have been sexually violated. Our relationship with the police is paramount.

My parents still live in Macclesfield as does my older brother Andrew with his own, almost grown up family, and Richard, whose early years were hampered not only by bad health, but also by a big sister whose anger and rebellion did nothing to ease his situation, is now a strong, healthy man living in Manchester with a beautiful wife and two young children.

I feel as if I should be telling you, in conclusion, that our lives, since that amazing day almost thirty years ago, have been a heady mix of happiness, laughter and joy. In the main, this is true and the life we have enjoyed has without doubt only been made possible because of what God did and has since done. I still, to this day, cry with gratitude and confess to never having got over the shock of discovering His reality. I hope I never do. Where would I be? I often ask myself. What would have happened to us? The answers are too unthinkable for me to imagine.

I'm so proud of my wonderful family. We have known much joy and been so grateful to belong to each other. I've seen Tom and Adam grow into strong, talented, faith-filled men, and they have each chosen beautiful, gifted wives who we love as our own daughters.

But belonging to God hasn't meant that we've never encountered problems, experienced hardships, pain and even heartbreaking loss. These past few years have, without doubt, been the most difficult of our lives, and it's no exaggeration to say that my faith has, at times, been stretched beyond breaking point. One day, when the time is right, this story too will be told. But in the meantime I cling to the knowledge that His strong, everlasting arms have held us steady and kept us intact through the storm. He has promised that nothing in life or death can ever separate any one of us from His love, His hope, and the promise of our eternal home.

This journey has for me, been emotional, intense, but above all strengthening. And although I have spoken of these events many times over the years, I have never before re-visited each step in such detail and with such scrutiny.

Did I hold my course? Did I find my way?

As I approach the close of this very personal account of my journey to faith, I find myself reminded once again, somewhere deep in my spirit, that all is well. God's beautiful, eternal Kingdom has neither changed nor moved its position. The first tender shoots of healing are just beginning to surface, and the immeasurable, invincible vastness of His love that stretches out beyond the shores of the universe remains as ever, in place. His perfect peace and tranquillity once again touch my inner being. I am home.

I waited patiently for the Lord,
And He inclined to me and heard my cry,
He brought me up out of the pit of destruction,
Out of the miry clay,
And He set my feet upon a rock making my footsteps firm.
And He put a new song in my mouth,
A song of praise to our God.

(Psalm 40 v 1-3, New American Standard)

We hope you enjoyed reading this New Wine book.
For details of other New Wine books
and a wide range of titles from other
Word and Spirit publishers visit our website:
www.newwineministries.co.uk
or email us at newwine@xalt.co.uk

Contacts

If you have been affected by any of the issues raised in this book, you may find the following contacts helpful:

Addaction
Leading specialist drug and alcohol treatment charity
www.addaction.org.uk
020 7251 5860

Frank
Friendly, confidential drugs advice
www.talktofrank.com
0800 776600

The Roofie Foundation
Dealing with drink spiking, drug rape and sexual abuse
www.roofie.com
0800 783 2980

Lifecentre
Supporting survivors of rape and sexual abuse
Office: 01243 786349
Helplines:
     Adults: 0844 847 7879
     Under 18's: 0808 802 0808
Text: 07717 989 022
email: help@lifecentre.uk.com
Web: www.lifecentre.uk.com

The Survivor's Network
Supporting female survivors of sexual violence and abuse
www.survivorsnetwork.org.uk
01273 203380

Sue Mills
You can contact Sue Mills via **www.sue-mills.com**